A Language Without Words

Michael Raattama Tripp

Many Raven Voices

An imprint of Raven Publishing, Inc.
Norris, MT

A Language without Words

Published by:
Many Raven Voices
Raven Publishing, Inc.
PO Box 2866
Norris, MT 59745

www.ravenpublishing.net

For Freya, family, and my mother, Alice

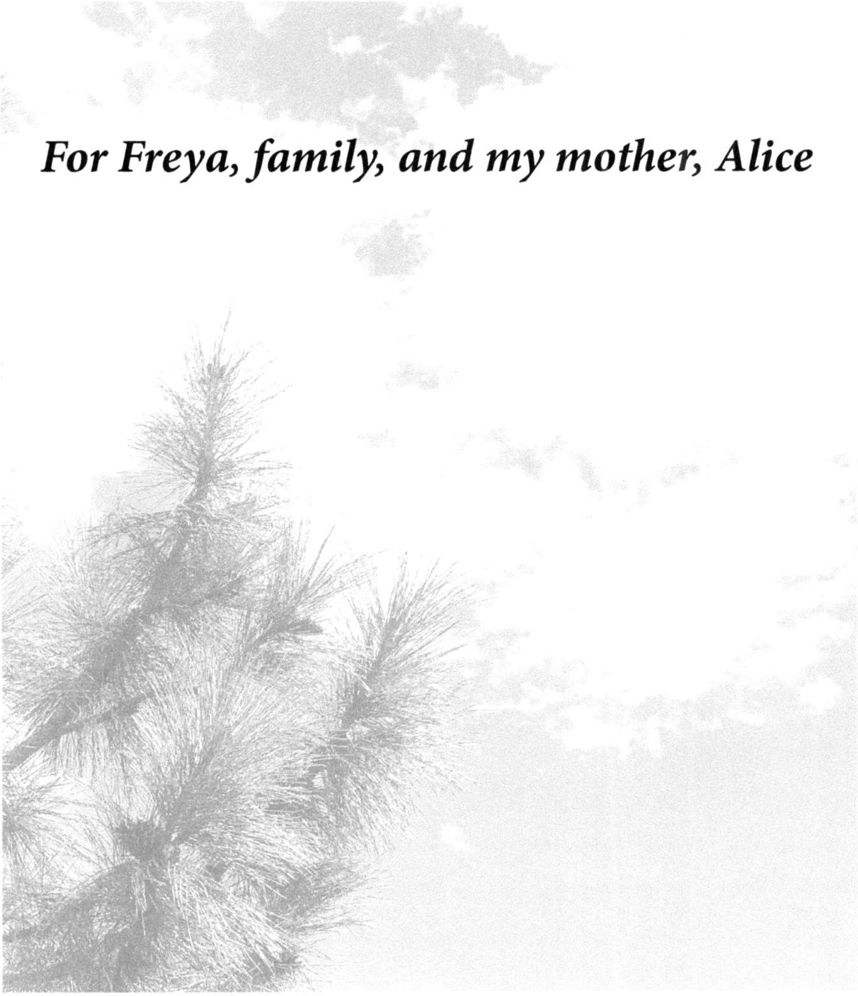

Credits

Ink drawings throughout are by © Freya Tripp.

Photographs are as follows:
Cover - Lake Scandinavia, Minnesota.
Waterfront at Tripp family cabin. Photo © by Freya Tripp.

Page 1: Deschutes River canyon during salmon fly hatch and mock
orange bloom, © by Tim Whitsel,
p 55: Deschutes River canyon © by Michael R. Tripp.

This work could not have been completed without the support and
thoughtful reviews by Tim Whitsel and Roger Sabbadini, and the
technical support of Janet E. Hill.

Foreword

These poems are a compilation of moments from my years, a memoir of sorts. As family and friends know, I am a listener, and only occasionally, the talker.

My appreciation of poetry goes to my earliest memories. Mother Alice loved to recite poems of the masters. Decades later when I would play a Dylan tune, she would recite lines from the poems Dylan had drawn on.

Over the years I was only occasionally moved to attempt to record a poetic thought or emotion, being consumed by life's activities as so many folks are. Mother was always an enthusiastic reader. Those poems that were saved are due to efforts of my lifelong mate Freya. Recently my sister-in-law, Anita, compiled writings that my mother, Alice, had filed away, typed on an old Underwood. And our children and grandchildren occasionally share their efforts. This has motivated me to compile my few writings. Hopefully they will have meaning for family and maybe for other readers who have experienced echoing moments. I hope my children, family, and grandchildren will find energy and time to record and share their creative voices.

Contents

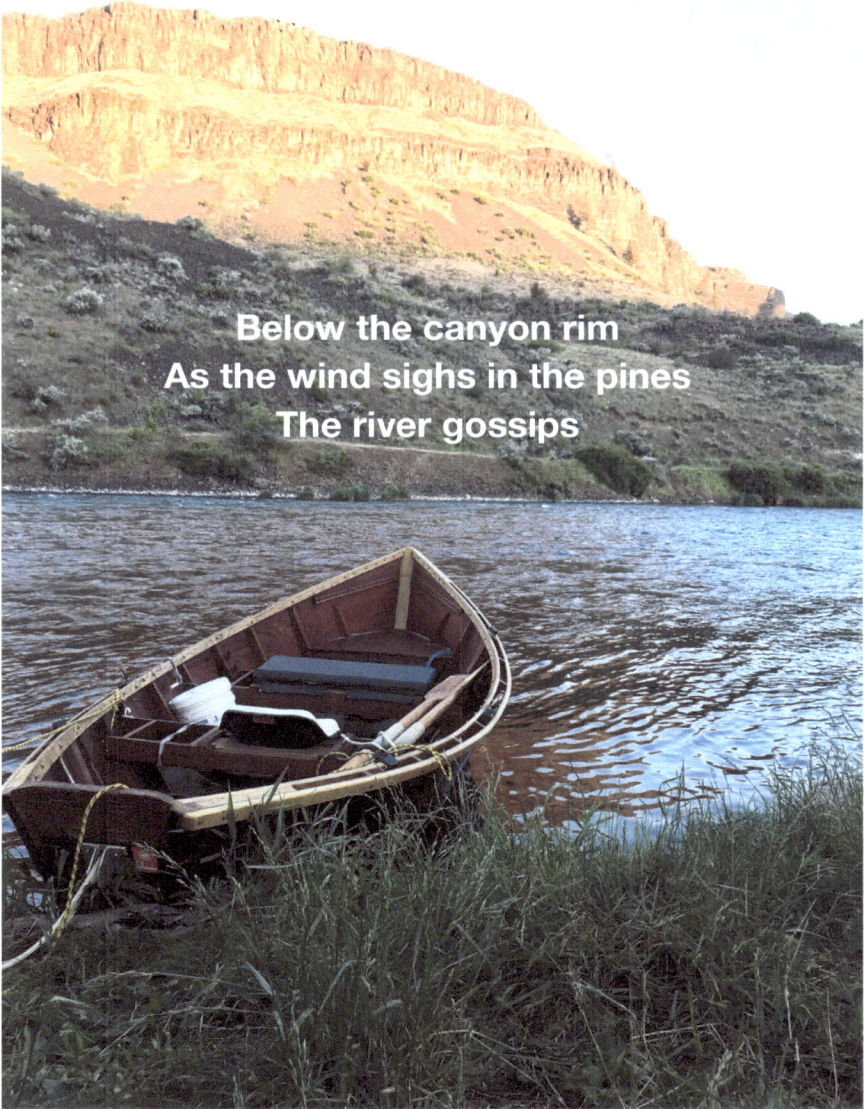

Below the canyon rim
As the wind sighs in the pines
The river gossips

Uitwaaien*

It is a short hike through scrub juniper
The foehn wind pushing
Down into the canyon where
    The ice rimmed river runs dark

Here clarity is found
Walking in the wind
    Uitwaaien

It is a short hike upriver
Through red twigs and willows
    The river bending to the solstice sun
        Green sprouts challenging the season

Here warmth is found
Walking in the wind
    Uitwaaien

*Uitwaaien (OUT-vwy-ehn) Dutch.
To walk in the wind, to take a
break to clear one's head.

2

January Rains

Dreams sculpt reality
Time swallowed in clouds
All on a day of rain

Surely in the misted hills
Sheltered from rain
Refuge can be found

There tales are told
Days of conquest
Conjured from wind driven rain

Yet valley fog holds mysteries
Born of rain
Hidden in the clamor of geese

Warmed by coffee   we wait
Waters will clear
Salmon will run

Early Spring

In early spring
There is a moment
Pressing on the afternoon
When the cusp of the season
Sits next to you
Asking what next

The sun's warmth
Belies the winter of yesterday
Stirring yearning
Challenging acceptance
Passing quickly into sunsets glowing

In these moments
Transition blurs
Uncertainty is intoxicating
Change certain

August in Minnesota

Of a leaf
Secure to hard oak bough
    Passing days of sun
Greeting evening storms

Bearded heads below
    Trembling
Whisper in heat

On the Road to Scandi

In sun sweated shell
I sat on a roadside
Surveying those passing

Sheltered in quiet
Stating my case
I conversed with death

Prairie Sunset

Ruby slings
Reach from far

Wrapping the steeds
Passing for reins
Eluding grasp
Of day sliding

Wrapping the shadows
Passing for ribbons
Denying sight
Of night dawning

Leaving Minnesota

Facing the blustery wind
I looked across the prairie
Thinking a young man
Had no need of goodbyes

Trees here reflect sweat
    Partitioning men's efforts
Where depth could only be
Clouds above the fields

There I lived the need
To brush the setting sun
Growing corn
Spiking nails

But on this shadowless afternoon
Buffeted by wind
    Ants and leaves settled in dust
I knew my time had passed

Evening in the Lake Scandi Cabin

Sometimes I dream
That my lack of wings
Must be an illusion

Surely I have been a cormorant
A black silhouette
Drooping feet
In labored progress

Or a heron
Stiffly stepping
Through shadows
In formal blue suit

Tonight a beetle
In paper armor
Charging the citadel
Desperate for light

Notes of the season
Call to each

In the symphony
Peace is found

Northwest Christmas

On lazy streams of light
Among assembled elders
An owl flew

Watching we held hands
Blanketed in our billowing breath
Warm in a wintering forest's quiet

Winter Solstice

At winter solstice
The sun crawls along the horizon
Hiding behind hills
Inching above tree tops
Seeking the western mountains

In the flat light
Of this reluctant orb
Life pulsates
A mélange of vibrant colors

On this shortest of days
There are no shadows

Snowshoeing

Snowshoeing the winter forest
Voices broken by crunching steps
A trail is opened

On our outings
In different years
And seasons
We have spoken of many things
Framing our mortality
In worn anxieties

In the suspended moment
Unbroken silence
We drift with the snow
Trees share inner conversations
Speaking of our journey
In softened tones

Snow Flurries

Snow flurries
Swirling in spring sun
Defy the moment
Of warm earth landing

Silence
    Not empty
Speaks to one's soul

Music
    Listen
Fills our sphere

Within calm waters
We are easily seduced
Breaking waves awaken

Prayer Flags

Prayer flags flutter valiantly
Speaking to the winter squall
Their bright colors bleached to grays
    Shredded
Incantations delivered on the winds

First strung after the avalanche
Prayers of desperation
    Embraced for solace
    Written in an ancient script
Renewed on the winds

Voices

We last spoke in early winter
Your youthful words of hope
Focused on tomorrow

Geese flew above the fog
A chorus of voices
Guiding us each onwards

With spring
Snow melted first under the bay window
Grasses greened then browned into summer

In the heat of evenings
I listened for your voice

With the return of the cold season
Snow blankets glow in the moonlight
The forest is quiet

In soundless snowfall
I listened for your voice

Walking the rim path again
Listening to the rushing voices
The river running deep in the canyon

I cry to hear your voice
To learn this language without words

Tumalo Rainbows

On this fall morning

Red leaves dropped by rain
Drift between lichens and
Verdant mosses

Sunglow
Through broken clouds
Birthing a rainbow

Arcing so close
I should have touched at least
The purples and blues

Landing behind the ridge
Where the creek runs cold
Where rainbow trout wait

Waiting for spring's thaw
Swimming on songs of the river

Kaleidoscope

Years ago in joy
Full patterns tumbled past
    The moment
The chips of a life
    An instant
Embraced in our memory

Dawn at the 32nd St. Apartment

Perched above the elms
I have watched the street
    Dawn to dawn
Never understanding

But this morning
Listening to the dawn chorus
    Shadows fading
An old woman approached

Dressed in black
She rested on her cane
And in foreign tongue
Explained

Tonight
I watch for her return
How to explain
    Sailing on prairie winds

On the Mississippi

On this quiet night

Standing by the river
Listening to the sounds
Fish feeding
Birds bold behind the darkness
Silent glass of flood

Cotton maidens seduce me

Crisp footsteps of man
Shatter the moment
Drowning the river

Inheritance

Communicating by fire
Mom sits in silence
Unanswered questions
Passed to her sons

Exam Morning at 32nd Street

Wisps of cotton
Limit my reach
Lock my muscles
My thoughts
In other worlds

Where time is
As I am not
And other selves
Deposing terrors
Recapture the womb

The council votes
I am the representative
Greeting the sunrise
Denying the clamor of horns
Seeking warmth of sleep in my coffee

Dreams

Once friends at dusk
Met without place
Sharing a city

Dreams were enough

When the dream died
Now alone
In a shadowed sun

I drew the curtain

The Joy of bluebirds
Dusting snow off juniper berries
Heralds the new year

Morning Sun

As the morning sun
Warms the alcove
The day yawns
Sheltered still space

The pure note of the solitaire
Patiently repeated
Breaks the spell
Herald the New Year

Red breasts and wax wings
Crowd for water
Drops flying in prismatic flashes
Icicles sparkling

In the turmoil of a winter thaw
The clamor of geese
Stirs primal urges
Echoes in the canyon

Sunset

As the sun sets
Cradled by white peaks in red clouds
Colors wash into grays

The canyon fills with shadows
Shades in the river roar
Voices unmuffled question

As the sun sets
Night sounds of the river
Question

Around the Campfire

Hunched in smoke
Fixated stare
Frozen face

Arriving youngsters
Shuffling slowly
Speak with their bodies
Sipping ales

Swirling smoke
Dancing with mosquitoes
The moment
Deepening into evening

In the new assemblage
His head rises
Words silently mouthed

As the line of cans lengthens
Fire stoked to flames
His life emerges

Children of his children
Speaking

The Coast this Winter

Rain drumming on the roof
Vacation at the coast
Reading an essay on mindfulness
A challenge to one's focus

Drumming rain
An invite to past memories
Embossed reflections

On this holiday
Where does this lead
Maybe key lime pie

Yet the floor trembles
The surf beyond the dunes
Pounds rhythms
Turbulence
Resonates with your realities

Drumming rain
Better finish that pie

Christmas Eve Pneumonia

One hopes this illness will pass
    Doesn't it usually
But in the lulls of a day in bed
One's imagination wanders
    Distressed dreams

Perhaps it is in these moments
That we accept reality provisionally

This evening
Remnants of the day
    Colored threads in the blanket's weave
Seem hidden
Perhaps discovered come morning

Waiting for Sunrise

In early morning
As snow banks glow
In full moon shadows
The wail of a train
Questions my presence

A call to run free
Forever relived when
The moon shines full

Now with passed time
Hiking the drive for the morning paper
Desires weigh heavily

In early morning
West of the mountains
The moon silvers into the glacier

Beach Stones

Blinking slowly
In wet sand sun
Birthed in the night's storm
From lands now vanished

Living in lucent colors
Stories of ancient fires
Wait to be told

Lummi Island

This sea is too quiet
Lights afar glimmering in the dark
Ships sinking from view

What sea is this
Without rumbling surf
Without tides

This sea is too quiet
To feel not alone
Lights glimmering too afar

Waves

The clarity of an empty glass
That simplicity
Somehow enough to reframe our conversations
A single breath

How to speak
Living in the moment
    Ambiguities, persuasions
Surrender

With the tide change
    We begin anew in washing waves
Shells at sea
    Dancing

Of a Twig

It was a twig
Somewhat distinguished in fact
Colorful lichen contrasting
Nicely with its nest of
Bitterbrush blooms

And there was a twinkle

Discovered the caterpillar
Pleading patience
Promised wings of bright colors
Flight on airs

The lodgepole forest chuckled
Calling this a fairy tale
A dead twig
Can't you see

Offended the twig crackled
Thrilled by its visitor
It offered to host a cocoon

Forest Voices

In the cacophony
Of the forest quiet
Questions are lost

My presence an anomaly
A whisper in the shadows
A rumor in the darkness

In the language spoken
Foreign to my ear
Concerns are voiced

Leaves are browned
Mosses curled
Buzzing bees absent

A moment of no words
My breath
An anomaly

Diamond Peak

Hiking for hours
In the soft autumn sun
We spoke little

Finally I rested by sheltering rock

She climbed on
Leading the children
Laughter echoing off the scree

The wind brings sounds of solace
Whispering grasses of summer picnic
Creaking bough of evening tryst

Moments past

In my aching muscles
Hot blood
I am

The Drive Home

Why on this day of usual
South hills showers
The motor humming
My soul speaks
I cannot say

Dissonant voices of youth
Vie in strident clamor
Exuberance past

Disengaged on arrival
The dialogue drifts
In the hissing silence of evening

Poetry Facilitation

With twilight
Tensions fade

Rambling to the dog
I explain why one distinguishes
Planets from stars
In the darkening sky

A crying infant
Rescues me from this discourse

Torn Coat

My coat is torn
I wear it still
Though the wind blows cold

Stretched and softened
By exertions past
It fits me well

Faded and bleached
Stained though washed
Its colors still warm

As evening shadows
I closet my coat
Wondering who knows me

Loreto Days

Warm breezes off tropical seas
Whispers in the palms
Seductions of solitude, aloneness

In the space of aloneness
It is yours, the moment
To celebrate or mourn

In aloneness is found space
Echoes of silence
Only your conversations

Breezes sigh, birds soar
Blueness of the depths
Your aloneness

No Socratic dialog this
Nor a quest for a transcendental utopia
Rather negotiations for a
Faustian bargain

What price for return to other waters
To feel prairie winds off the lake
Sauna warmed, cabin abuzz
Haunted voices

An Old Man

It is a profile of an old man
Hunched shoulders, bulging waist
Strong jaw, penetrating gaze

    You, or is it I
Perhaps we should pray

The prayer flags are tattered
Words now born on mountain breezes
    Unfulfilled hopes

Yet birds fly on seasons' winds
Songs voiced in confidence
Delivered beyond

The prayer flags flutter
Intent wavering, message faded
How should we pray

The congregation has gathered
Shared worlds spoken, homily heard
When will we pray

    You, or is it I
Time to pray

John Day Canyon

The night is cold
Depthless shadows
Sublime loneliness

Burnt canyons
Landscapes lost
Cathedrals with ashened altars

In protest the river murmurs

In dialogs of campfire smoke
I listen for your voice
It has been too long since we spoke

Your mother and I miss your counsel
Life's journey cannot fill your absence
    Give us guidance
       Travel well

Autumn at Lake Scandi

The time is late
Aching muscles, wheezing breath
Unfinished work

Lake breezes arouse

In this place of growing
Foundations were laid, walls raised
Unions were celebrated, poems penned
Words never spoken

Fall begs forbearance
Leaves turned
Sunset gray on the waves
Hopes foundered

In the evening gathering
Sunflowers sing the mantra tornasol
But who will greet the sunrise
Who will write the eulogy
When will it be read

Spring Thaws

For a while
A moment already past
The wind is ours

Of whites and grays
Spring thaws
To summer basks

In Pursuit of Happiness

Faint and nauseous
Looking in vain for shade
Heat mirages obscure upstream camp sites

With each step
The decision to chase Deschutes steelhead
This day challenged

Stumbling into camp
Cool waters found
Lapping waves to ease fatigue

As shadows deepen the
Need to plumb the waters
Line was cast on riffles

Cooled by midnight airs
Breaks hold steelhead
In sleep's confused dreams

Trembling ground arouses
    Not a dream
Thin tent no shield from the intrusion

Screeching metal
Pounding engines on stressed rails
Canyon invasion full blown

Sanctuary breeched
Fate of the waters unclear
Steelhead undaunted swim,
     spawning imperative

Still the morning star beams
Perched on the canyon rim
Serenely indifferent to the contrail-laced sky

On Finding Mother's Poems

Dried roses rest quietly
Dust from years past
Lending mystery to their stories
That vase from Goodwill
Nestled in the towel basket
From a simpler life

Mother included flowers in
Poems of her later years
Color and lightness in reflections on
Aging, not always cheering
    Regrets inevitable in a caring life
Bouquets not sent to her mother

Now my years
On review
Look for moments of light
Blooming roses of spring
Glimmering reds of autumn maples
Past still present
    In balance, hauntings
    Bouquets not sent

For Alice Raattama Tripp
August 22nd, 1918 - September 11th, 2014

The Farm at Springhill

It was with the turn of black soil
Plowing the fields
That I first understood father
    His desire to work the land

In that year's drought
Watching thunderstorms roll off the prairie
We stood with him, praying for rain
    To restore the land

With shortened days of autumn
Harvesting corn and beans
We worked through dusk
    Golden fields over the land

In winter
Then and now
Gathered in the kitchen
    We murmur of Spring's coming

For John Gilbert Tripp
September 3rd, 1919 - March 6th, 2014

Elegy for a Riverman

In the manner of a resolute man
Entering the rapid
Measured strokes, efficient pulls
Commitment is clear

> Running the river
> Following light into dusk
> Kawaakari*

Sounds resonate with the setting sun
In the river's roar, Ponderosas moan in the wind
Hammering from an unseen ranch
Challenging cries of osprey

At day's end
Swooshing nighthawks search mirrored riffles

> Running the river
> Sunsets of flowing water
> Kawaakari

Kawaakari (Japanese 川明かり)
pronunciation (ka-wa-a-ka-rE)
The glow of a river or stream at dusk,
The gleaming surface of a river

www.ingramcontent.com/pod-product-compliance
Lightning Source LLC
LaVergne TN
LVHW010016070426
835511LV00001B/2